DIVERSITY, EQUITY, and INCLUSION CURRICULUM

By Mary Birdsell and Jo Meserve Mach

FINDING MY WORLD
The Finding My World book series presents nonfiction, multi-cultural, and geographically diverse books that give voice to children with disabilities. Inclusive stories offer students the opportunity to meet children and adults with disabilities.

DEI CURRICULUM
With the social acclaim that 'Everyone Matters' it is important for students to learn about diversity, equity, and inclusion (DEI). As a literature-based study, this curriculum promotes DEI skill development by fostering student exposure to individuals living around the world with disabilities and expanding their capacity to build relationships with all their peers.

© 2021 Mary Birdsell, Jo Meserve Mach

These activities may be reproduced solely for classroom use and may not be used or posted online.

Finding My World DEI Curriculum

Finding My Way Books
3512 SW Huntoon St.
Topeka, Kansas 66604
www.findingmywaybooks.com

(785) 273-6239

ISBN: 978-1-94754-132-0

Printed in the United States

10 9 8 7 6 5 4 3 2 1

For more information or to contact the author, please go to www.findingmywaybooks.com.

DEI CURRICULUM — FINDING MY WORLD BOOK SERIES

The **Finding My World** book series presents nonfiction, multi-cultural, and geographically diverse books that give voice to children with disabilities. Inclusive stories offer students the opportunity to meet children and adults with disabilities.

Each lesson within this curriculum links two books to explore a different competency. Students will gain context for each competency by reading the stories, learning background information, answering discussion questions, and completing activities.

Diversity, Equity, and Inclusion

Competencies are the skill, knowledge, abilities, and behaviors that describe the standard to which a competent person is expected to perform…seven primary competencies associated with diversity equity, and inclusion:

- *Understanding Implicit Bias*
- *Microaggression Development and Understanding*
- *Cultural Competency*
- *Promotion of Civility*
- *Social Justice Development*
- *Organizational Learning*
- *Youth Development*

dei.extension.org

ABOUT THE CO-AUTHORS AND PHOTOGRAPHER

Mary Birdsell has authored nine children's books and is a former Speech and Theatre teacher with an enthusiasm for all styles of learners. Mary believes everyone learns, creates, and has a story to tell. As a photographer, she strives to create images that reflect the strengths of each child. Mary's background in education, theater, and photography intersects as she visually creates books. She uses colors and shapes to tell a story. For her, each book is like its own theater production.

Jo Meserve Mach is co-author of the Finding My Way book set. She is very passionate about sharing the stories of children with special needs after 36 years of working as an Occupational Therapist. Jo embraces the joy individuals with disabilities bring to our communities through their unique gifts.

Finding My World book series: DEI Curriculum

Table of Contents

Neema Wants to Learn and ***Claire Wants a Boxing Name*** 1

    Paying Attention 3

    What Happens Next? 4

    Helping a Friend 5

    Being Claire's Inclusive Friend 6

Matteo Wants to See What's Next and ***MyaGrace Wants to Get Ready*** 7

    What Does Your Face Say? 9

    Being MyaGrace's Inclusive Friend 10

Cooper Wants to Do Chores and ***Onika Wants to Help*** 11

    Growing Vegetables and Caring for Sheep 13

    My Bookmark 14

    Cooper's and Onika's Book Report 15

    Being Onika's Inclusive Friend 16

Claire Wants a Boxing Name and ***Matteo Wants to See What's Next*** 17

    Understanding How to Talk with Your Eyes 19

    Being Matteo's Inclusive Friend 20

MyaGrace Wants to Get Ready and ***Cooper Wants to Do Chores*** 21

    It's Great to be Included 23

    Let's Start a Book Club 25

    Being Cooper's Inclusive Friend 26

Onika Wants to Help and ***Neema Wants to Learn*** 27

    Reader's Theater Script and Discussion 28

    Being Neema's Inclusive Friend 33

Finding My World DEI Activities Key 34

Inclusive Friend Award 36

DEI CURRICULUM

NEEMA WANTS TO LEARN
CLAIRE WANTS A BOXING NAME

Genre: Nonfiction
GRL: M
Interest level: K-4
Lexile: 470L

Genre: Nonfiction
GRL: M
Interest level: K-4
Lexile: 470L

DEI competency: understanding implicit bias

Disabilities represented: learning disability, differently sight-abled, facial difference

Themes: diversity, equity, inclusion, women, attention

The **Finding My World** book series presents nonfiction, multi-cultural, and geographically diverse books that give voice to children with disabilities. Inclusive stories offer students the opportunity to meet children and adults with disabilities.

Introduction
Neema and Claire both have supportive women in their lives. Orphanage director Mama Mdemu is supportive and helps Neema learn as she tries new things. Claire's mother is supportive of her using her abilities to be involved in many activities.

Neema models her actions after Mama Mdemu as she learns to play ball, grate a coconut, and help the younger children.

Claire's coach, Vivian, is differently sight-abled and has a service dog. Vivian is an amazing woman and teaches Claire how to focus as she learns to box.

Diversity is a fact. Equity is a choice. Inclusion is an action. Belonging is an outcome. David Robertson

Diversity
Neema is 11 years old, has a learning disability, and lives in Tanzania. Claire is 10 years old, has a facial difference, and lives in Canada. Vivian immigrated from Hong Kong and lives in Canada.

Equity
Neema gets to go to school. Tanzania has often limited schooling to boys. Claire goes to the Toronto Newsgirls Boxing Club, and it is equal to any men's boxing club.

Inclusion
Neema likes to play with her friend Joseph and take care of the younger children. Claire does competitive cheerleading.

"Savoy Howe's Toronto Newsgirls Boxing Club was born from her experiences in aggressive, male-dominated boxing gyms, but it was much more than just a place to work out. The club became known as a safe space for survivors of domestic violence and the LGBTQ+ community — a place where women-identifying members could realize their strength and speed bags were adjusted for people who used wheelchairs. For 24 years, Howe's gym introduced boxing to people who may have been too intimidated to try it otherwise." besthealthmag.ca

DEI CURRICULUM

NEEMA WANTS TO LEARN
CLAIRE WANTS A BOXING NAME

Discussion Questions

1. What do remember about reading *Neema Wants to Learn*?
2. What do you remember about reading *Claire Wants a Boxing Name*?
3. What do Neema and Claire have in common?
4. How do Neema's and Claire's stories show strong women?
5. Are there jobs that women can't do? Explain.
6. What makes people think that different jobs are only for certain people (stereotypes)? Explain.
7. How do those types of attitudes or stereotypes make you feel? Explain.
8. How does understanding different attitudes help you understand people? Explain.
9. Can you name any women who have worked against stereotypes (Harriet Tubman, Kamala Harris, etc.)?
10. What do you admire about women who have worked against stereotypes?

WHAT IS IMPLICIT BIAS?

"…implicit bias refers to the attitudes or stereotypes that affect our understanding, actions, and decisions in an unconscious manner. These biases, which encompass both favorable and unfavorable assessments, are activated involuntarily and without an individual's awareness or intentional control."
Kirwan Institute at Ohio State University

Activities

Paying Attention
This activity reviews what Neema learned from Mama Mdemu and what Claire learned from Vivian. The emphasis is on what you can learn by paying attention to what others are doing.

What Happens Next?
Students imagine what happens next in either Neema's or Claire's story.

Helping a Friend
This activity teaches students how to approach and to help someone who has visual impairments. It empowers them to be an inclusive friend of someone who is differently sight-abled.

Being Claire's Inclusive Friend
This activity encourages inclusive thinking. Students identify three things they have in common with Claire and three ways they could play together.

DEI competency: understanding implicit bias

Neema Wants to Learn and Claire Wants a Boxing Name

Paying Attention

Name_____   Date_____

Neema and Claire both have strong women in their lives. They paid attention and learned from them.

Neema watches Mama Mdemu. Put an X in front of what she learned from Mama Mdemu.

_____How to plant a garden

_____How to play the game Catch

_____How to grate apples

_____How to sing a song about pineapples

_____How to grate coconuts

_____How to sing a song about coconuts

List one more thing Neema learned from Mama Mdemu.

_____

Claire watches Vivian. Put an X in front of what she learned from Vivian.

_____ How to do the Can Opener

_____ How to do the Blender

_____ How to wrap her hands for boxing

_____ How to do pullups

_____ How to do pushups

_____ How to hit a boxing bag that looks like a peanut

List one more thing Claire learned from Vivian.

_____

DEI competency: understanding implicit bias

Neema Wants to Learn and Claire Wants a Boxing Name

What Happens Next?

Name_____   Date_____

1. Write a sentence about what happens next in either *Neema Wants to Learn* or *Claire Wants a Boxing Name*. **Your sentence needs to show inclusion.**

    You can write about what Neema does next.

    Or you can write about what Claire does next.

    _____

    _____

2. Draw a picture of what happens next. It should go with your sentence.

DEI competency: understanding implicit bias

Neema Wants to Learn and Claire Wants a Boxing Name

Helping a Friend

Name_____ Date_____

When Claire goes to the boxing club for her lessons, Savoy, the owner, gives her a special training. Since her coach Vivian is differently sight-abled, Savoy teaches Claire how to assist Vivian so she can walk safely around the boxing club without her service dog.

Savoy taught Claire to put her arm at her side and brush up beside Vivian, so Vivian knows where she is.

Vivian taught Claire that they are like magnets. Vivian attaches herself to Claire's arm and moves with her.

Find a partner and take turns being Claire and Vivian. When you are Vivian, you need to wear a blindfold or keep your eyes tightly closed.

Write a sentence describing how it feels to be Claire.

_____

_____

Write a sentence describing how it feels to be Vivian.

_____

_____

Find a new partner and take turns following these directions on how you approach someone to offer help.

> **Tips for helping people who are blind or have low vision**
>
> 1. Approach: if you suspect **someone** may need a hand, walk up, greet them and identify yourself.
> 2. Ask: "Would you like some **help**?"
>   The **person** will accept your offer or tell you if they don't require **help**.
> 3. Assist: listen to the reply and **help** as required.
>
> visionaustralia.org

DEI competency: understanding implicit bias

Claire Wants a Boxing Name

Being Claire's Inclusive Friend

Name_____   Date_____

After reading Claire's book, think about what you have in common with her. Think about how you might play together if she came to visit. When you share time with someone and include them in activities, you are learning to be an inclusive friend.

Three ways I am just like Claire:

1. _____
   _____

2. _____
   _____

3. _____
   _____

Three ways I would have fun with Claire:

1. _____
   _____

2. _____
   _____

3. _____
   _____

DEI competency: understanding implicit bias

DEI CURRICULUM

MATTEO WANTS TO SEE WHATS NEXT
MYAGRACE WANTS TO GET READY

Genre: Nonfiction
GRL: M
Interest level: K-4
Lexile: 490L

Genre: Nonfiction
GRL: N
Interest level: K-4
Lexile: 530L

DEI competency: youth development

Disabilities represented: cerebral palsy, intellectual disability

Themes: diversity, equity, inclusion, communication

The **Finding My World** book series presents nonfiction, multi-cultural, and geographically diverse books that give voice to children with disabilities. Inclusive stories offer students the opportunity to meet children and adults with disabilities.

Introduction

Both Matteo and MyaGrace are being taught to respect all people. They Know people with disabilities. Matteo has a close family friend with a disability. MyaGrace has a disability and has friends with disabilities.

Matteo spends the day visiting a local museum where his family friend Rebecca is a docent. She has cerebral palsy and uses her eye gaze to show Matteo and his brother Cristian the exhibits.

MyaGrace is very excited about getting ready to attend a school dance. She has to decide what to wear, her hairstyle, and her nail color.

Diversity is a fact. Equity is a choice. Inclusion is an action. Belonging is an outcome. David Robertson

Diversity

Matteo's friend Rebecca has cerebral palsy, is nonverbal, and uses a wheelchair. Matteo lives with his brother and parents in Canada.

MyaGrace was born in India and adopted by an American family. She had difficulty learning to eat when she was young. She is small for her age. MyaGrace has cerebral palsy and intellectual disabilities.

Equity

Matteo has grown up with Rebecca as a close family friend. His family considers her to be no different from their other family friends. MyaGrace's parents expect her to be part of the family as much as her three siblings.

Inclusion

It is important to both Matteo's and MyaGrace's families that they include others with different type of abilities in their lives.

DEI competency: youth development

DEI CURRICULUM

MATTEO WANTS TO SEE WHATS NEXT
MYAGRACE WANTS TO GET READY

Discussion Questions

1. What do you remember about reading *Matteo Wants to See What's Next*?
2. What do you remember about reading *MyaGrace Wants to Get Ready*?
3. What do Matteo and MyaGrace have in common?
4. How do Matteo's and MyaGrace's brothers help them?
5. What is it like to have a sibling?
6. How do you communicate with your siblings (or friend, if no siblings)?
7. What can make communicating with your siblings challenging (or friend, if no siblings)?
8. How do siblings change who you are?
9. How can siblings help you become the best you can be?
10. Why do you want to become the best you can be?

WHAT IS YOUTH DEVELOPMENT?

"...recognizes, utilizes, and enhances young people's strengths; and promotes positive outcomes for young people by providing opportunities, fostering positive relationships, and furnishing the support needed to build on their leadership strengths." *Interagency Working Group on Youth Programs*

Activities

Museum Visit
See how a museum can be accessible and inclusive. Visit the museum in Matteo's story, the [Royal Ontario Museum](#) and explore [online exhibits](#).

What Does Your Face Say?
This activity emphasizes how we can talk to each other without using our voices. Have students practice using their expressions to communicate.

Being MyaGrace's Inclusive Friend
This activity encourages inclusive thinking. Students identify three things they have in common with MyaGrace and three ways they could play together.

Matteo Wants to See What's Next and MyaGrace Wants to Get Ready

What Does Your Face Say?

Name_____   Date_____

Rebecca uses her eye gaze and her facial expressions to communicate. MyaGrace also uses her facial expressions to communicate. Actually, so does Matteo and so do you! Our facial expression tells others how we feel all the time.

Say nothing. Instead, move your body as you share these feelings. You can practice in front of a mirror or with a partner. Put a check mark in the box when you have figured out the expression.

☐ I'm glad.

☐ I'm disappointed.

☐ I'm sad.

☐ I'm mad.

☐ I'm confused.

Have a conversation with a partner. Take turns being the person to ask the questions. When you answer the questions, only use a facial expression. Here are some ideas for questions.

How do you feel about going outside?

How do you feel about going on vacation?

How do you feel about missing lunch?

How do you feel about losing your homework?

How do you feel about going to the game?

DEI competency: youth development

MyaGrace Wants to Get Ready

Being MyaGrace's Inclusive Friend

Name_____   Date_____

After reading MyaGrace's book, think about what you have in common with her. Think about how you might play together if she came to visit. When you share time with someone and include them in activities, you are learning to be an inclusive friend.

Three ways I am just like MyaGrace:

1. _____

_____

2. _____

_____

3. _____

_____

Three ways I would have fun with MyaGrace:

1. _____

_____

2. _____

_____

3. _____

_____

DEI competency: youth development

DEI CURRICULUM

COOPER WANTS TO DO CHORES
ONIKA WANTS TO HELP

Genre: Nonfiction
GRL: N
Interest level: K-4
Lexile: 520L

Genre: Nonfiction
GRL: M
Interest level: K-4
Lexile: 480L

DEI competency: cultural competency

Disabilities represented: intellectual disabilities, autism, arthrogryposis, TAR syndrome

Themes: diversity, equity, inclusion, sustainability

The **Finding My World** book series presents nonfiction, multi-cultural, and geographically diverse books that give voice to children with disabilities. Inclusive stories offer students the opportunity to meet children and adults with disabilities.

Introduction
Cooper and Onika both have disabilities and their homes are rural. Cooper helps his family raise sheep. Onika helps her friend Teo take care of a vegetable garden. Both are helping our world become more sustainable.

Cooper's family raises sheep for wool that helps in clothing production.

Onika and her friends are learning how to help their village. Teo is raising vegetables to help feed the village. Elibeth and Agnes are learning to cook. Onika is making jewelry to sell and help fund their school.

Diversity is a fact. Equity is a choice. Inclusion is an action. Belonging is an outcome. David Robertson

Diversity
Cooper has arthrogryposis and TAR syndrome. His family lives on a farm in a rural US community. The village where Onika lives is in a rain forest in Tanzania. She has intellectual disabilities.

Equity
Cooper attends a public school for all children. Onika attends a school that is only for children with disabilities. It is important they both can go to school. Cooper and Onika know they want to be treated like other students so they can take part in all school activities.

Inclusion
Cooper has spent many months of his life receiving medical care and understands the feeling of being separated from others. He wants to be included in whatever is happening.

When Onika was young, the culture of her community required all children with disabilities to be hidden. She wants to go to school and learn skills so that others in her village will see her as part of their community.

DEI competency: cultural competency

DEI CURRICULUM

COOPER WANTS TO DO CHORES
ONIKA WANTS TO HELP

Discussion Questions

1. What do you remember about reading *Cooper Wants to Do Chores?*
2. What do you remember about reading *Onika Wants to Help?*
3. What do Onika and Cooper have in common?
4. How do Onika and Cooper work differently on farms?
5. What is it like to work on a farm?
6. How is working with animals and plants the same? How is it different?
7. Why are farms important?
8. What makes living on a farm different from living in a city?
9. How is where you live a part of your culture?
10. Is one culture more important that another? Why or why not?
11. Why is it good to be around different cultures?

WHAT IS CULTURE COMPETENCY?

"...the ability to understand, appreciate and interact with people from cultures or belief systems different from one's own."
apa.org

Activities

Growing Vegetables and Caring for Sheep
This activity encourages students to contrast the care of animals and plants.

My Bookmark
Discuss culture and how Cooper and Onika present different cultures. The activity encourages students to think about their own cultures. Different cultures are part of diversity. It's fun to learn about different cultures.

Cooper's and Onika's Book Report
A fill-in-the-blank book report form helps students identify their feelings, recall what each story is about, and reflect on the cultures presented.

Being Onika's Inclusive Friend
This activity encourages inclusive thinking. Students identify three things they have in common with Onika and three ways they could play together.

DEI competency: cultural competency

Cooper Wants to Do Chores and Onika Wants to Help

Growing Vegetables and Caring for Sheep

Name_____ Date_____

Sustainability

Onika and Cooper both live in places that care about sustainability. They take care of earth's natural resources and help our planet to be healthy.

Where is their work done? Draw a line from the task to the garden or the barn.

dig dirt with hoe

scoop grain

scatter seeds

push dirt into piles

mark lambs with paint

trim hooves

scoop dirt

fill feed bunk

give sheep medicine

Think about tools that are used to do the work (one tool could be used for both).

Put a V in front of the tools you need to grow vegetables.

Put an S in front of the tools you need to take care of sheep.

_____scoop

_____pitchfork

_____plunger

_____hoe

_____hoof trimmer

_____bucket

DEI competency: cultural competency

Cooper Wants to Do Chores and Onika Wants to Help

My Bookmark

Name_____   Date_____

Everyone's family has something they like to do together. This is part of their family culture. Cooper takes care of sheep with his family. What does your family like to do together?

Cut out your bookmark. Decorate it by drawing a picture of your family's culture.

DEI competency: cultural competency

Cooper Wants to Do Chores and Onika Wants to Help

Cooper's and Onika's Book Report

Name_____   Date_____

When I read Cooper's book, I felt _____ because
_____.

When I read Onika's book, I felt _____ because
_____.

The best part of Cooper's story is when _____
_____.

The best part of Onika's story is when_____
_____.

I learned _____

_____ about the culture where Cooper lives.

I learned _____

_____ about the culture where Onika lives.

DEI competency: cultural competency

Onika Wants to Help

Being Onika's Inclusive Friend

Name_____   Date_____

After reading Onika's book, think about what you have in common with her. Think about how you might play together if she came to visit. When you share time with someone and include them in activities, you are learning to be an inclusive friend.

Three ways I am just like Onika:

1. _____
_____

2. _____
_____

3. _____
_____

Three ways I would have fun with Onika:

1. _____
_____

2. _____
_____

3. _____
_____

DEI competency: cultural competency

DEI CURRICULUM

CLAIRE WANTS A BOXING NAME
MATTEO WANTS TO SEE WHAT'S NEXT

Genre: Nonfiction
GRL: M
Interest level: K-4
Lexile: 470L

Genre: Nonfiction
GRL: M
Interest level: K-4
Lexile: 490L

DEI competency: promotion of civility

Disabilities represented: cerebral palsy, differently sight-abled, facial difference

Themes: diversity, equity, inclusion, role model

The **Finding My World** book series presents nonfiction, multi-cultural, and geographically diverse books that give voice to children with disabilities. Inclusive stories offer students the opportunity to meet children and adults with disabilities.

Introduction
Claire and Matteo both live in urban Canada. Also, both have the experience of being friends with an adult who is living successfully with a disability.

Claire takes boxing lessons from Vivian, a woman who is differently sight-abled and has a service dog. Matteo has grown up with his mother's friend Rebecca, who has cerebral palsy and is very active in her community. Matteo spends a day with Rebecca exploring the biodiversity area of the Royal Ontario Museum. Rebecca uses her eye gaze to direct the visit.

Diversity is a fact. Equity is a choice. Inclusion is an action. Belonging is an outcome. David Robertson

Diversity
Claire and Matteo live in a bilingual world of English and French. They are both bilingual. Vivian is an immigrant from Hong Kong and has a service dog named Catcher. Rebecca uses a wheelchair and is nonverbal. She communicates primarily through her facial expressions and eye gaze.

Equity
With community and family support, Vivian and Rebecca are working or volunteering as responsible adults living full lives with friends.

Inclusion
Both Vivian and Rebecca are active participants in their communities. Vivian has Catcher's support to negotiate public transportation. This enables her to teach boxing, lead community yoga classes, and entertain others with her music and comedy acts.

Rebecca's mother assists her. Rebecca takes part in community programs that offer her opportunities to dance, paint, and care for plants. She uses PowerPoint presentations to advocate for others with disabilities.

DEI competency: promotion of civility

DEI CURRICULUM

CLAIRE WANTS A BOXING NAME
MATTEO WANTS TO SEE WHAT'S NEXT

Discussion Questions

1. What do you remember about reading *Claire Wants a Boxing Name*?
2. What do you remember about reading *Matteo Wants to See What's Next*?
3. What do Claire and Matteo have in common?
4. What do Vivian and Rebecca have in common?
5. What does Vivian teach Claire?
6. What does Rebecca teach Matteo?
7. What is a role model?
8. Why is it good to have a role model?
9. How is being a role model a part of Vivian's and Rebecca's identities?
10. How do you show respect for a role model?
11. Would you want Vivian or Rebecca to be your role model?
12. Who could be your role model? Why?
13. Why is it important to acknowledge other peoples' strengths?

WHAT IS CIVILITY?

Civility comes from the Latin word *civilis*, meaning "relating to public life, befitting a citizen," in other words, being friendly and nice to everyone. **When you show civility, you use kindness and good manners**. You are respectful, even if you do not like that person very much. *Civility* can also mean formal politeness, like your behavior at a fancy dinner. *Vocabulary.com*

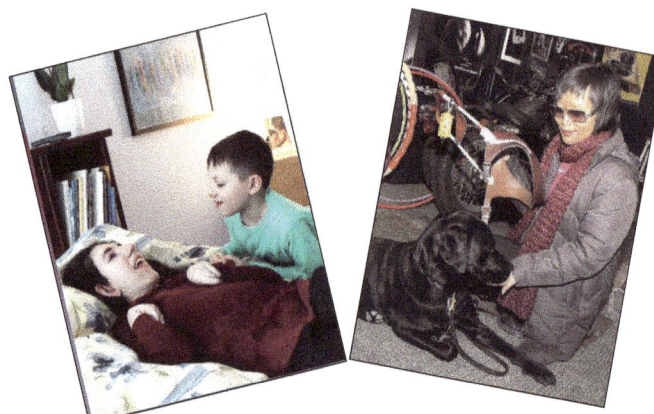

Activities

Understanding How to Talk with Your Eyes
This activity gives students the opportunity to practice using their eyes to talk to someone.

Learn More About Rebecca
Visit Rebecca's [website](#).

Music Video
Watch and listen to members of the French-Canadian band [Les Trois Accords](#) (The Three Chords) sing in French.

Being Matteo's Inclusive Friend
This activity encourages inclusive thinking. Students identify three things they have in common with Matteo and three ways they could play together.

DEI competency: promotion of civility

Claire Wants a Boxing Name and Matteo Wants to See What's Next

Understanding How to Talk with Your Eyes

Name_____   Date_____

 In Matteo's book, Rebecca uses her eye gaze to direct Matteo and Cristian through the exhibits they visit. Are you surprised she can do that? Do you think it would be hard to do?

Let's see if you can talk with your eyes.

Find a partner to be your buddy. Cover your mouth. Use your eyes to say the words in each box below. Have your buddy circle the words you say the best with your eyes.

 Take a walk with your buddy and use your eyes to `tell' your buddy where you want to go. Do not use your hands to give directions. Only use your eyes!

Circle the words that best describe how you feel when you're using your eyes to talk.

happy   sad   confused   mad   frustrated   silly   excited

DEI competency: promotion of civility

Matteo Wants to See What's Next

Being Matteo's Inclusive Friend

Name_____   Date_____

After reading Matteo's book, think about what you have in common with him. Think about how you might play together if he came to visit. When you share time with someone and include them in activities, you are learning to be an inclusive friend.

Three ways I am just like Matteo:

1. _____
   _____

2. _____
   _____

3. _____
   _____

Three ways I would have fun with Matteo:

1. _____
   _____

2. _____
   _____

3. _____
   _____

DEI competency: promotion of civility

DEI CURRICULUM

MYAGRACE WANTS TO GET READY
COOPER WANTS TO DO CHORES

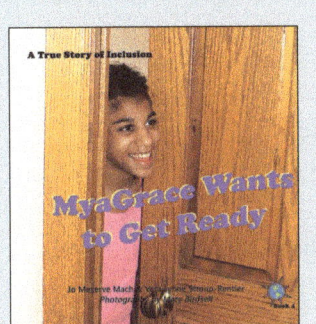

Genre: Nonfiction
GRL: N
Interest level: K-4
Lexile: 530L

Genre: Nonfiction
GRL: N
Interest level: K-4
Lexile: 520L

DEI competency: promotion of civility

Disabilities represented: cerebral palsy, intellectual disabilities, arthrogryposis, TAR syndrome

Themes: diversity, equity, inclusion, family

The **Finding My World** book series presents nonfiction, multi-cultural, and geographically diverse books that give voice to children with disabilities. Inclusive stories offer students the opportunity to meet children and adults with disabilities.

Introduction
MyaGrace and Cooper both have a disability and live in the United States. MyaGrace lives with her family in a town. Cooper lives with his family on a farm.

MyaGrace's family supports her as she follows her interests in dance and music to attend a school dance. Cooper helps his family complete all the chores they do to take care of the sheep they raise.

Diversity is a fact. Equity is a choice. Inclusion is an action. Belonging is an outcome. David Robertson

Diversity
MyaGrace was born in India and adopted by her American family. When she was young, she had difficulty learning to eat. She is small for her age. MyaGrace has cerebral palsy and intellectual disabilities.

Cooper has spent his life receiving a lot a medical care as his physical disabilities have required surgery and therapy. Cooper has arthrogryposis and TAR syndrome.

Equity
Both MyaGrace's and Cooper's families treat them as an equal participant in their families. Their parents expect them to contribute to what their family is doing, just like they expect their siblings to contribute.

Inclusion
MyaGrace's story is about a peer inviting her to a school dance that includes all the students in the school. It is not about a special needs school dance that is only for children with special needs.

Cooper's parents want him to be successful. His dad assists him as needed, but encourages him to help with their chores.

DEI CURRICULUM

MYAGRACE WANTS TO GET READY
COOPER WANTS TO DO CHORES

Discussion Questions

1. What do you remember about reading *MyaGrace Wants to Get Ready*?
2. What do you remember about reading *Cooper Wants to Do Chores*?
3. What do MyaGrace and Cooper have in common?
4. How would you describe MyaGrace?
5. What is MyaGrace's family like?
6. How would you describe Cooper?
7. What is Cooper's family like?
8. Why is it important to support your family members?
9. Is it okay to be different from your family?
10. What makes families strong?

WHAT IS CIVILITY?

Civility comes from the Latin word *civilis*, meaning "relating to public life, befitting a citizen," in other words, being friendly and nice to everyone. **When you show civility, you use kindness and good manners**. You are respectful, even if you do not like that person very much. *Civility* can also mean formal politeness, like your behavior at a fancy dinner. *Vocabulary.com*

Activities

Discussion
Facilitate a classroom discussion encouraging students to share how the members of their families work to include them in community activities. Here are examples: an older sibling drives them to a sport practice game or their parents take them to the park so they can play with their friends.

It's Great to Be Included
These activities review how MyaGrace's and Cooper's families include them in their family activities.

Let's Start a Book Club
This fill-in-the-blank form guides the discussion for the students' first book club meeting.

Being Cooper's Inclusive Friend
This activity encourages inclusive thinking. Students identify three things they have in common with Cooper and three ways they could play together.

DEI competency: promotion of civility

MyaGrace Wants to Get Ready and Cooper Wants to Do Chores

It's Great to be Included

Name_____   Date_____

Being included is very important to Cooper and MyaGrace. Compare how their families include them.

Use the words in the box to fill in the blanks. Each sentence describes how Cooper is being included.

cat	medicine
grain	pitchfork
hay	plunger
hoof	side

Cooper pushes the _____ with the side of his hand to squirt the

_____ into the lamb's mouth.

Dad grips the lamb's hoof. Cooper scrapes the _____ of the

_____.

Cooper fills the feed bunk with _____.

Cooper uses the _____ to pitch _____ to the sheep.

Cooper feeds the _____ all by himself.

DEI competency: promotion of civility

MyaGrace Wants to Get Ready and Cooper Wants to Do Chores

It's Great to be Included

Name_____   Date_____

Being included is very important to Cooper and MyaGrace. Compare how their families include them.

Use the words in the box to fill in the blanks. Each sentence describes how MyaGrace is being included.

color	Mom
dances	ready
Ethan	shimmers
list	sparkles

Mom helps MyaGrace make a _____ of what she needs to do to get _____.

MyaGrace shows _____ the dress she likes.

MyaGrace chooses a dress that _____ and _____.

MyaGrace _____ with _____ to try out her new shoes.

MyaGrace chooses the _____ of her nail polish.

DEI competency: promotion of civility

MyaGrace Wants to Get Ready and Cooper Wants to Do Chores

Let's Start a Book Club

Name_____   Date_____

To start your book club, have everyone read MyaGrace Wants to Get Ready. Then get together. Answer these questions as you talk about the book.

What was the book about? _____

_____

_____

What did you like about the book? _____

_____

_____

What do you think happens next? _____

_____

Which person in the story would you like to know more about? _____

What would you like to know? _____

What is an example of a family member showing civility during the story? _____

_____

_____

DEI competency: promotion of civility

Cooper Wants to Do Chores

Being Cooper's Inclusive Friend

Name_____   Date_____

After reading Cooper's book, think about what you have in common with him. Think about how you might play together if he came to visit. When you share time with someone and include them in activities, you are learning to be an inclusive friend.

Three ways I am just like Cooper:

1. _____
   _____

2. _____
   _____

3. _____
   _____

Three ways I would have fun with Cooper:

1. _____
   _____

2. _____
   _____

3. _____
   _____

DEI competency: promotion of civility

DEI CURRICULUM

ONIKA WANTS TO HELP
NEEMA WANTS TO LEARN

Genre: Nonfiction
GRL: M
Interest level: K-4
Lexile: 480L

Genre: Nonfiction
GRL: M
Interest level: K-4
Lexile: 470L

DEI competency: social justice development

Disabilities represented: intellectual disabilities, autism, learning disabilities

Themes: diversity, equity, inclusion, identity

The **Finding My World** book series presents nonfiction, multi-cultural, and geographically diverse books that give voice to children with disabilities. Inclusive stories offer students the opportunity to meet children and adults with disabilities.

Introduction

Onika and Neema are both girls with disabilities growing up in Tanzania. Onika lives with her family and attends the Rainbow School. Her village built it for children with disabilities. Onika's story shares her experiences of learning at her school.

Neema lives in an orphanage and attends a community school that provides both a basic education and training for her to become a childcare worker. Her story shares all the interesting experiences she has on a typical Saturday.

Diversity is a fact. Equity is a choice. Inclusion is an action. Belonging is an outcome. David Robertson

Diversity

Onika is a teenager with intellectual disabilities who has attended school only as an adolescent. She is interested in color, design, and creating jewelry. Neema is an 11-year-old girl with learning disabilities who is growing up in a community setting and helping care for younger children. Her interest is in becoming a teacher.

Equity

Both Onika and Neema may attend school. Their communities have given them the opportunity to learn about their abilities and work toward reaching their full potential. In Tanzania, girls and children with disabilities are much less likely than boys to be given the opportunity to get an education.

Inclusion

Onika and Neema take part in all the activities at their schools. They are both learning skills that will help them contribute to the needs of their communities when they are adults. This creates a way for them to be included.

DEI competency: social justice development

DEI CURRICULUM

ONIKA WANTS TO HELP NEEMA WANTS TO LEARN

Discussion Questions

1. What do you remember about reading *Onika Wants to Help*?
2. What do remember about reading *Neema Wants to Learn*?
3. What do Onika and Neema have in common?
4. How does school look different in Tanzania compared to where you live?
5. What does Onika's school do that is special?
6. How does Neema's school work help her?
7. What does your school do to help you learn?
8. Does everyone get a chance to learn in your school?
9. Do you think everyone gets a chance to learn all over the world?
10. How does going to school help you be the best you?

WHAT IS SOCIAL JUSTICE?

The objective of creating a fair and equal society in which each individual matter, their rights are recognized and protected, and decisions are made in ways that are fair and honest. *Oxfordreference.com*

Activities

Discussion and Research
Encourage students to share their knowledge of their family members or others in their community did not get social justice.

when

Ask students to vote for the social justice incident they would like to research. Upon completion of the research project, have students write a report and submit it to a local media outlet.

Reader's Theater Script and Discussion
This activity gives students the opportunity to act out Onika's story. Use the questions for audience interpretation and discussion.

Being Neema's Inclusive Friend
This activity encourages inclusive thinking. Students identify three things they have in common with Neema and three ways they could play together.

DEI competency: social justice development

Onika Wants to Help

Onika Wants to Help: Reader's Theater Script

Roles: Narrator, Onika, Valentine, builders, Teo, Elibeth, Agnes (Two or more students could share *Narrator* role.)

Props: Rainbow School sign, hoe, watering can, bucket, carrots, two bowls of rice, art area, string, beads

Settings: school, garden, kitchen, art room

NARRATOR: This is a story about Onika who lives in Africa.

    She lives in a rainforest in the mountains.

    She lives in a small village in Tanzania.

ONIKA: My name is Onika. *(Onika stands by Valentine, who is doing schoolwork.)*

    I like bold colors. I like pretty things.

    When I was a little girl like Valentine, I didn't go to school.

    I learn differently from other children.

    Adults in my village thought I should stay at home.

    I didn't get to be part of my village.

NARRATOR: As Onika grew older, everything changed. *(Builders make school with Rainbow School sign.)*

    The villagers built a new school.

    They built it for children who learned differently, like Onika.

    In the morning, the students at school do schoolwork.

    In the afternoons, they learn to do different jobs.

    Let's meet some of Onika's friends from school.

TEO: My name is Teo. *(Teo is working in a garden.)*

    I love to work in the garden.

    I have a talent for growing vegetables.

NARRATOR: Teo likes to use a hoe.

    He likes to get the dirt ready to plant.

    He thinks it's fun to plant seeds.

    He likes to get water for the plants.

Onika Wants to Help

TEO: I'm learning to take care of plants.

I grow carrots, cabbage, spinach, garlic, and green peppers in the garden.

ONIKA: *(Onika and Teo work together in the garden. Onika collects carrots.)*

I like to help Teo gather carrots.

It's fun to work together.

But this isn't my talent.

There's something else I love to do.

NARRATOR: What do you think Onika loves to do?

What do you think is Onika's talent?

Let's meet more of Onika's friends.

NARRATOR: Elibeth and Agnes love to prepare food. *(Elibeth and Agnes sit with bowls of rice.)*

They have a talent for cooking.

They buy rice from the market.

Then, they search for dirt on the rice.

AGNES: My name is Agnes.

I think it's fun to swish the rice in the bowl.

ELIBETH: My name is Elibeth.

I like to clean the rice.

NARRATOR: Elibeth and Agnes are learning to prepare food.

While they work, they talk and laugh.

ONIKA: Sometimes, I help Elibeth and Agnes. *(Onika washes carrots in the bucket.)*

It's fun to work together.

But this is not my talent. There's something else I love to do.

NARRATOR: What do you think Onika loves to do?

What do you think is Onika's talent?

She likes to help in the garden.

She likes to help prepare food.

But she loves to do something else.

(Again, the Narrator asks audience to guess what Onika loves to do.)

Onika Wants to Help

ONIKA: This is the art room. *(Onika sits at a desk with beading supplies.)*

This is where I like to be.

I love working with beads!

My talent is making jewelry. *(Onika works on a beaded necklace.)*

NARRATOR: Onika loves all the colors.

She gets to pick the beads she wants to use.

She scoops up the beads.

She has to be very careful.

She has to look closely as she works.

ONIKA: *(Onika shows the pattern of the necklace she is making.)*

I love to show how different colors go together.

NARRATOR: The school sells the jewelry Onika makes.

The money helps their school buy supplies.

ONIKA: I'm learning how I can help our village. *(Onika holds up the finished necklace.)*

Someday, I will make money for our village by selling my necklaces.

TEO: I am learning how I can help our village. *(Teo stands with his hoe and watering can.)*

Someday, I will grow plants for our village.

ELIBETH: We are learning to help our village. *(Elibeth and Agnes stand with their bowls of rice.)*

AGNES: Someday, we will help prepare food for our village.

NARRATOR: *(Onika, Teo, Elibeth, and Agnes stand in front of the Rainbow School sign.)*

Onika and her friends are very happy.

They are learning to help their village.

They are thankful for their school.

Their school helped them find their talents.

Onika Wants to Help and Neema Wants to Learn

Reader's Theater: Discussion Questions for Audience Interpretation

1. How is Onika's school like your school?

2. How is Onika's school different from your school?

3. Would you like to go to a school like Onika's?

4. Why do you think schools are different in different parts of the world?

5. Should schools be the same everywhere?

6. Onika's friends all like to do different things. Is that the same for your friends?

7. Is it okay for friends to like different things?

8. Onika and her friends are all learning things to help their village, their community. What have you learned to help your community?

9. Is it good to help the community?

10. What kind of jobs help the community?

11. Which of these jobs can you do?

DEI competency: social justice development

Neema Wants to Learn

Being Neema's Inclusive Friend

Name_____   Date_____

After reading Neema's book, think about what you have in common with her. Think about how you might play together if she came to visit. When you share time with someone and include them in activities, you are learning to be an inclusive friend.

Three ways I am just like Neema:

1. _____

2. _____

3. _____

Three ways I would have fun with Neema:

1. _____

2. _____

3. _____

DEI competency: social justice development

Neema Wants to Learn and *Claire Wants a Boxing Name*

Paying Attention Activity

X for Neema:

- how to play the game Catch
- how to grate coconuts
- how to sing a song about coconuts

X for Claire:

- how to do the Blender
- how to do pushups
- how to hit a boxing bag

MyaGrace Wants to Get Ready and *Cooper Wants to Do Chores*

It's Great to Be Included Activity for Cooper

Cooper pushes the **plunger** with the side of his hand to squirt the **medicine** into the lamb's mouth.

Dad grips the lamb's hoof as Cooper scraps the side of the **hoof**.

Cooper fills the feed bunk with **grain**.

Cooper uses the **pitchfork** to pitch **hay** to the sheep. Cooper feeds the **cat** all by himself.

It's Great to Be Included Activity for MyaGrace

Mom helps MyaGrace make a **list** of what she needs to do to get **ready**.

MyaGrace shows **Mom** the dress she likes.

MyaGrace chooses a dress that **shimmers** and **sparkles**.

MyaGrace **dances** with **Ethan** to try out her new shoes.

MyaGrace chooses the **color** of her nail polish.

Finding My World book series: DEI Activities Key

Cooper Wants to Do Chores and *Onika Wants to Help*

Growing Vegetables and Caring for Sheep Activity

Garden:
  dig dirt with hoe
  scatter seeds
  push dirt into piles
  scoop dirt

Barn:
  scoop grain
  mark lambs with paint
  trim hooves
  fill feed bunk
  give sheep medicine

V:
  hoe
  bucket

S:
  scoop
  pitchfork
  plunger
  hoof trimmer

Finding My World Certificate

Diversity, Equity, and Inclusion

Inclusive Friend Award

For building an inclusive community one friend at a time!

Awarded to

_____

_____

Signature and Date